The Indie Author's Guide to:
Building a Great Book
by graphic designer and indie author Jo Michaels

The Indie Author's Guide to:

Building a Great Book

By Jo Michaels

Print Edition

Copyright 2012 Jo Michaels

License Notes

Published by Jo Michaels.

ISBN-13: 978-1478206224

ISBN-10: 1478206225

Author's Note:

Before we begin, let me tell you the basic things you will need to format your book by these guidelines. If you have another program you're more familiar with, use that. This book is meant to be a guide only.

I reference Adobe Photoshop for building covers in *The Indie Author's Guide to Building a Great Book*. If you use Gimp or some other image manipulation software and know where the panels I discuss in this book are, use your program.

I reference Microsoft Word 2007 for formatting interiors in *The Indie Author's Guide to Building a Great Book*. If you know how to do the things outlined in this book in another program and prefer it, use yours.

In most of this book, I'm assuming you have a basic working knowledge of your chosen program and are familiar with tabs and menus.

I'm passing on knowledge that will help your book appear more professional in the mass market. Period.

My expertise lies in the field of Graphic Design and a lot of what you'll find here imparts knowledge I learned during my studies and things I have discovered on my own while publishing my books. I spent a year as a Graphic Design tutor and was chosen amongst the other graduates in my final year to design the commencement cover (they loved it so much they used it again the following year).

I've listened to common complaints people have about self-published books and tried to address those areas here as well so we all look like we went to design school and have worked at a big publishing house our whole lives (or at the very least, that we can play with the big boys – and do it *well*).

Section six is the longest section because consideration of a print version of your book requires a lot of work. Follow me once and keep me around for a quick reference guide.

You may ask me additional questions via Twitter @WriteJoMichaels if you feel compelled to do so.

If you indulge in banging your head on the desk or tearing out your hair while reading this book (the very thing I'm trying to help you avoid – bald authors with red foreheads make us all look nuts), I take no responsibility. Enter at your own risk, and enjoy!

Table of Contents

Section One – Branding Yourself

I cannot stress this point enough. You *must* brand yourself if you are an author – indie or otherwise. Think about those big companies out there.

What do they all have in common? Branding.

McDonalds has those golden arches, Coca ~ Cola has that red can and special font, and AT&T has the globe.

This section will explain how to brand yourself with books, blogs, and everything digital. You need to do it. Yes, it's a PITA. But *so* worth it! If you want to be successful, you'll read on and put this advice into action.

Choosing an Identity

What is an identity? Easy answer: it's what identifies you and sets you apart from every other author out there. Slightly more difficult answer: it's a set of rules you use anytime you publish, post, mail, or blast anything. It's the font, color scheme, layout, and possibly logo. It's your constant. Examples of identities I have designed:

http://jomichaels.blogspot.com/p/identity-packages.html

When someone sees one of your books on the shelf, your blog post, your e-mails, your letterhead, or your business card, they should think: *I know that author!*

You don't have a business card? Oh my. We'll touch on that now.

As an author, consider using something other than a standard business card. See if you can find a designer that will make you amazing bookmarks that can be cut (or that tear) to standard business card size. After all, you want to be able to fit into that rolodex. Believe it or not, a *ton* of people still use a rolodex. Oversized business cards are an interesting idea but they cannot be punched and inserted. Those cute little seed packet business cards are great if you want your card planted and forgotten about. Avoid kitschy. If you're giving your card to a reader, what better way to let them find your new books than by giving them a bookmark they can keep and use (and look at) forever?

A business card is typically part of an identity package that most designers set a flat fee for. You get a business card, letterhead, and an envelope as part of the deal. Note that this package rarely includes a logo design. That's a whole separate monster! Speaking of logos…

Creating a Logo (or having one created for you)

A logo should be something that defines you in one glance. You're more than an author, right? A vast majority of us are also parents, artists, photographers, bloggers, etc… Your logo should speak to your soul. It should be a huge part of you. If you don't love it, reject it.

You may want to use the letters of your name to create a logo or a specific image. You can create a logo on your own following these simple steps:

1. Consider what you love
2. Think about the letters in your name (or pen name)
3. Don't think about color because your logo needs to work in black and white
4. Think small

Sketch it out then pass it on to an artist you know or a designer for fleshing out. Having a logo created by a designer costs more than rendering one from an existing artwork.

Keep the following advice in mind if you're designing one yourself:

1. Don't use a tiny series of lines (when scaled down, they become a blob)
2. Your logo should work at 1/4

3. Don't use tiny artwork with tiny holes (they close up as well)
4. Be bold – sometimes less and smaller is better than more and bigger

Color schemes come *after* logo design.

Color Scheme Dos and Don'ts

Do:

- Choose colors that are harmonious. There are so many tools out there to help you accomplish this task! Please, use them! This one is my favorite:

http://kuler.adobe.com/#create/fromacolor

And will provide you with hours of entertainment dragging the handles around the screen. Not only that, it will give you the RGB, CMYK, LAB, and HEX colors. You can't beat that.

- Choose only two colors plus black. Your printing costs will be off the charts if you choose more than two.

If you don't like that website, use a color wheel. You can find one rather inexpensively at most art stores.

Take a moment and remember what I'm about to tell you. There are three primary colors – red, blue, and yellow, three secondary colors – orange, green, and violet, and six tertiary colors – red-violet, blue-violet, blue-green, yellow-green, red-orange, and yellow-orange. Look at a color wheel:

http://jomichaels.blogspot.com/p/color-wheel.html

Notice the relationships between the colors. *Never* forget it.

Don't:

- Go color crazy. If you're dead set on that neon green, choose a nice, light, milk chocolate brown or a soothing, pastel, pink cream to go with it.
- Use clashing colors or colors that alter other colors when in proximity. For example, a red surrounded by a green is going to make the red look super red.
- Assume all this is bull and ignore my suggestions completely.

Consistency is Queen – *Because Kings are controlled by Queens!*

Now comes the difficult part of putting it all into action. You have your logo, your color scheme, and your font choices (more on why that matters later). After all that is settled, your responsibility is now to make sure it stays consistent. Remember, you're branding here. Do you ever see the McDonalds sign in neon green? No. There's a reason for that.

Use your selected colors on your blog, business cards, e-mail layouts, fliers, websites, *everything*. Because, chances are, you just spent a lot of time figuring it all out and making decisions. If you don't love the decision or the design, reject it. Crystal Lee and I went through three cover designs before we hit on one she loved. We never gave up.

It's your business product and it needs a flawless face. Never *ever* think about letting it slide this *one* time. Chances are that one time you ignore your identity will end up being what people see the most of. Murphy's law and all that jazz.

I'm going to tell you a super secret now: your website will fall into place after all that branding and fit in like it was designed just for you. There is really no need to pay $3,000+ to have a designer go in and build it for you. You need a web person at this point. Give them your branding constants and they will shock you. If you're doing it yourself, just stay with your identity and you'll be shocked at what you get.

Section Two –
Formatting Your Manuscript

Dos and Don'ts when Writing Your Book

Use normal for your style always. You can go back and change things after. Trust me on this; you want every piece of your text in normal style. Your headings and such are easier to change after you type your manuscript.

If you took a typing class in high school, forget everything you learned but the position of the keys. NO double spaces after periods and DO NOT tab at the beginning of a paragraph. I'm not a Scrivner lady but I know MS Word and I know what e-readers will do to your manuscript if you use tabs or double spaces after periods.

You already tabbed and double spaced, you say? Oh my. Well, fear not! Here's a link that will save you hours of headaches:

http://www.writersblockadminservices.co.uk/5-little-known-tips-to-improve-your-ebook-formatting/

Pop on over, tell my friend, Jo Harrison, I said, "Hello!" and thank her for posting that priceless information. You can also hire her to do all this annoying formatting *for* you! She's a virtual assistant, too. Cool, right? No, I don't get paid for references.

Don't put extra carriage returns between your paragraphs. Yuck. It gaps out big-time on an e-reader. Use the paragraph panel instead.

Choose wisely for your font. Not every font will show up on an e-reader! Stick to the basics like Times New Roman, Calibri, Cambria, or Arial. Use the same font in all of your books. Remember that thing about consistency being queen?

Quick Tips for Better Legibility

Consistency is queen but content is king. You can turn their heads only to disgust them when they open your book and attempt to read it. First off, hire an editor. Here's one I know personally and I know she'll treat you well:

http://www.writemarketdesign.com/

Her name is Laura Orsini and you can tell her I sent you. No, I don't get kickbacks!

Once your manuscript is beautiful and error free, continue on.

Here's where we get a little tricky. When you format for an e-book, you use a very different approach than when you format for a print version. I'll go into print versions later on and the best choices for those. Let's focus on the e-reader versions for now. Mkay?

You already know which fonts to choose from because of the lovely list I provided, but what else is there to think about?

1. Point size – how big your font is
2. Leading – the lines between your sentences
3. Kerning – the space between your characters

Determining number one will lead to determining numbers two and three. You all know what a point size is so I won't bore you with that. Leading should always be your point size plus two (at a minimum). Word does this pretty well on its own. Notice that when you change the point size and hit enter, the spaces between your lines get bigger. Ah ha! That's why! Yes. It is. It's so your first line of text has ample space for the line under it to sit freely without touching. Bingo! You got it!

Proper font size for an e-reader is 12pt. If you want to go smaller, don't go below 10pt. Bigger? Don't go above 14pt (I have broken that rule in headings *only* throughout this book). Remember that people can change the font size on most readers so what you choose matters little but a 16pt font will appear *huge* when scaled up on a reader. This *does* apply to your *title* page as well.

Determining leading and kerning is something best left for your print version. That's later in the book (section six). If you're working on a print version, feel free to skip down.

Building Your Save System

This is one of the most important steps in keeping your files organized. Create a master folder called something like Book Files and individual folders inside for each title and publication avenue. I will give you an example of mine.

Desktop>Books, Writings, Etc…

Inside my Books, Writings, Etc… folder I have each of the following:

Abigale
Yassa
Player
Mystic
Stuff I have started one chapter of
Smashwords
CreateSpace
Kindle
NOOK

Inside Abigale:

Book One
Book Two
Book Three
Cover Designs

Each of those folders has a folder for research, outlines, and notes.

Inside Smashwords:

Abigale Book One
Yassa

This is so I can find what I'm looking for without giving myself a headache. If I want to find the .doc for the final version of *The Abigale Chronicles – Book One*, I go to:

Desktop>Books, Writings, Etc...>Abigale>Book One>Chapters>The_Abigale_Chronicles_Book1_JoMichae ls_Final.docx

It makes it easy and lessens confusion.

Now I will discuss naming your files just in case you misplace one.

Always use underscores and the whole title including the draft number. You may even want to add the date on the end. Why? Wellll, when you do a search on your computer, it makes it easier to find what you're looking for if you name them appropriately. You'll be thanking me someday.

Consider this: if I called all Chapter 1 files Chapter 1 and I save it in the wrong folder, how the hell can I ever be expected to find it again? I can't. I thought I saved it to the Abigale>Book One>Chapters directory but what if it was in

Yassa>Chapters?! What if I saved over my Yassa Chapter 1?! Exactly. Just do it.

Different Formats for Different Platforms

Every platform you publish to needs a different file type. This is why Smashwords has seen such wild success! They take your .doc or .docx file and do all those pesky conversions *for* you with their meatgrinder program. You need to follow Mark Coker's *Smashwords Style Guide* to the letter or you're going to end up with a very big headache. That little book also walks you through creating a linked Table of Contents for your word file. I'll provide the links to everything later on.

However, *if* you want to do it yourself, there are things you need to know:

> ➢ Kindle prefers .html
> ➢ NOOK prefers .epub
> ➢ CreateSpace wants either a .doc or a .pdf
> ➢ Smashwords wants a .doc or a .docx

Now, most of them will take your .doc and convert it on site. You don't really want to do this because you need to be able to control your output. Take charge and take responsibility for creating great content.

If you publish with Smashwords, you can opt out of distribution to Amazon and Barnes & Noble and do them yourself.

For your Kindle version, save your final file out as usual in the folder Kindle>Book Title then save it again as an .html in the same folder.

For your NOOK version, save your final file out as usual in the folder NOOK>Book Title then save it again as a .rtf in the same folder. Then open Calibre (link later) and open your file. Click on Convert Books in the nav menu. Select epub as your output file and fill in all the blanks. Go to the Table of Contents section and check the box next to: Do not add detected chapters to the Table of Contents. If you followed *The Smashwords Style Guide*, your ToC will be in place already. Click OK on the bottom of the page. Click Save to Disk in the nav menu and save accordingly.

CreateSpace is a whole other animal. I'll go over that in section six so I'm not repeating myself and so you don't get confused.

Smashwords requires a bit of different formatting. While Kindle and NOOK will recognize page breaks, the meatgrinder needs a bit more (like extra carriage returns between chapters). If you go that route, follow Mark's book *to the letter*.

Section Three –
Building a Digital Cover

Size **IS** Important!

Most people will tell you size doesn't matter. Well, forget that mantra when it comes to cover art for your book. In the digital world, size is everything.

It's safe to build your file at no less than 3,000 pixels on the long side at 330dpi. If you don't know how to resize, that's okay. Most of the platforms will resize it automatically. Work in RGB color space for your digital cover. I'll go into print junk later. Create your digital file at the size you want your eventual book cover to be. You can thank me later when I show you how easy it is to create a print cover from a digital one that is built properly.

If you use Adobe Photoshop, when you create a new project, make sure your measurements are on inches. Here's where the math is a little tricky. I'll discuss bleed and what it means later, but for this purpose, let me give you a little tip: add 1/4" to the size of the cover you desire. If you want to print at 5.5" x 8.5" set the new project up to be 5.75" x 8.75" (that's a 1/4" addition).

Make sure your dpi is set to 330 and your digital file should be the perfect size for your print file. Please be careful with colors. I will go into that later as well when we discuss CMYK (the standard for print). Leave a little extra space on the left side for the print cover design due to binding and overlap.

Images

If you use images on your cover, I *beg* you not to swipe them offline. Go pay for them through the proper channels and get the rights. If you use a cover designer, make *sure* they have done the same thing. While places like 99Designs are great for cheap work, you end up paying for it in royalties to photographers if you aren't super duper careful.

Make sure you get the large version of the photograph. Pixilated (squarish) images look like crap when scaled up. If you get a photo at the same or nearly the same dpi with at *least* 2500 pixels on the longest side, you should be safe.

When you open the photo, do a quick conversion to black and white (remember that a lot of covers still show up that way) and make sure the details aren't lost. While landscape photos are gorgeous in color, you often lose the very thing that makes them gorgeous when they are converted. I'm a photographer as well as a designer, I know of what I speak. Okay? Moving on…

Font Choices – Why does it Matter?

Here we are again with fonts. There are a few things you need to know before you start designing your little heart out:

1. Kerning – the spacing between letters (professional designers spend *hours* tweaking this)
2. Free Fonts are never a good idea
3. Consistency is Queen
4. Remember the scaling down rule

Here's a little note before we continue: go look at Fern Michaels' books. Her titles are small, but her name is *huge*. Why? Because she *is* her brand.

Okay, time to get into the above. If you want to know how to kern, follow along.

Kerning in Adobe Photoshop:

1. Type out your words.
2. Note the areas where there is a little more space than you might want between letters.
3. Select the *preceding* letter then go to window>character and the little box will pop up like a magic wand that will allow you to adjust the spacing.

After that, follow the instructions here:

http://jomichaels.blogspot.com/2012/05/design-lesson-number-1-kerning.html

for a full on walkthrough of the next steps with purdy pictures for your enjoyment. Remember, this is an e-book first so I'm trying to avoid images within text. You'll get a link if I need to show you something.

Use your eyes. When it *looks* right, it *is* right. This is your baby and genetics have nothing to do with its face. You can sculpt and mold it however you see fit. Yay!

Free fonts are a bad idea because they rarely have built-in kerning pairs. True type fonts do. If you want to be super unique, go buy a font set to use or have someone render you a few words by hand, but remember that if you pay less than $30 for a font, it's probably worth exactly what you paid. Free fonts are also oftentimes copyrighted. Huge nono. If you use one and the font designer finds out, you're in for a lawsuit. Oops.

Consistency is queen because you already have your identity. Make sure you use the same font for your name every time you publish a doggone book. I cannot stress this enough. Content is king but your brand is what turns the eye your way.

Remember the scaling down rule because a heavy font's bowls (any open part of a letter, like the inside of an O) sometimes fill in when scaled down. Thin fonts disappear. Curly or decorative fonts can sometimes get confusing at a tiny size.

Before you go bananas, read the entirety of section SIX. Good tips in there!

Using Layers

This section is for anyone using Adobe Photoshop (or similar) or Adobe InDesign. When you add a new element to your design, put it on a new freaking layer. Don't you *dare* merge them together until you save it out as a .jpeg. Save that .psd and do *not* save over it. If you change something later, call it version 2. You can thank me later.

Layers in a design program are the same as paper layers. They allow you to rearrange elements (bring to front, back, etc…) as well as delete the element you have decided you don't want any more without buggering up your whole design. I have seen many designers save over their layered versions only to have to go back and re-do the whole project from scratch because they flattened an image or merged their layers.

Bad practice! Don't do it!

When you have designed to your heart's content and everything is just the way you want it, save your file then go to save as and choose .jpeg. It will ask you if you want to flatten your image, say yes. If you have any hidden layers, it will ask if you want to delete them, say yes.

Yay! Your cover is done! If you followed this guide, you're on your way to a print version very soon!

Again, be sure that you read section SIX before you put elements on that page that won't print right!

Section Four –
Final Checks

Uploading and Proofing

If you've gotten this far through the book, you've done all the editing work on your book and prepped your cover. You should be ready to upload your files to whatever distributor you choose. I will discuss my *personal* experiences with each and give you a little bit of information about another via another author I know that used a distributor on the list that I have no personal experience with. You need horse's mouth here.

If you don't have accounts with pubit, kdp, or any distributor of your choice, go sign up now. You have a lot of virtual paperwork to fill out. I'll wait…

Okay, done with that? Now it's time to upload those files you've worked so hard on! So log in and get to uploading!

Things You'll Need

Epub previewer:
http://www.barnesandnoble.com/u/nook-for-pc/379003591
Kindle previewer:
https://kdp.amazon.com/self-publishing/help?topicId=A3IWA2TQYMZ5J6

Other Things You'll Need (links)

Calibre: http://calibre-ebook.com/
The Smashwords Style Guide:
https://www.smashwords.com/books/view/52

Section Five –
Business Considerations

Choosing your distributor(s)

Here's where I tell my own story and allow my friend to tell hers. I distributed the first of my books with Smashwords only. My publication date was 4-25-2012 and I didn't get approved for premium distribution (iPad, Sony, B&N, etc…) until 5-18-2012 and I still wasn't showing on Amazon by the beginning of June. That was no good for me. My largest market was sunk! I opted out of Amazon and published there myself within a few hours. As of today 7-4-2012, my cover still isn't showing on Barnes & Noble. It's too late to pull it from there now.

CreateSpace was *fast* in their approval for my files and very specific when I had an issue. CreateSpace gets two huge thumbs up for that.

My second publication went much more smoothly. I opted out of distribution to B&N and Amazon and did them myself. My Smashwords version got uploaded on 6-3-2012 and was approved for premium distribution on 6-22-2012 and is already showing in iBooks as of 7-4-2012. I went live on Amazon after just twelve hours, live on B&N after twelve hours, and live on CreateSpace after eight hours.

My third publication went to KDP Select for 90 days so only got uploaded to Amazon and CreateSpace. It went live after ten hours.

Crystal Lee (over at http://crystalleeauthor.wordpress.com), author of the Canopy series, gave me her experience with BookTango:

My favorite thing about BookTango.com is how user friendly it is. Their editor is simple to navigate and correcting errors for the most part is a snap. It was also very easy to set up the table of contents. I used FreeTango, so it didn't cost me anything at all. I chose to go with BookTango.com for several reasons. The main one being that they distribute to so many retailers: Amazon, Barnes and Noble, Apple, Kobo, Scribd, Books on Board, Sony, and Google. I also liked that I retain my rights as the author so I can continue to shop around to other publishers. I took advantage of a promotional deal and will receive 100% royalties indefinitely. They do give 100% of net royalties, so that is something I found attractive as well. I didn't have to create a title page or copyright page either. They do that portion.

Now for the downsides: I disliked that they didn't have a find function key in their editor, so when I spotted errors as I went along on my original document, it was a pain to find it on the BookTango website in the body of the novel. There were also some problems with bolding. It would glitch out on me. Sometimes it would work, and sometimes it wouldn't. I found that a little frustrating and finally just gave up and didn't bold anything at all. It took about three days to get a link for my book. And they never did send me a direct email. They didn't even send me the link on their dashboard private messages on the website. I got it through a tweet from one of their employees. I thought that was kind of unprofessional. It took 3 days, so it wasn't a bad wait time. I also wish their website would retain my password at least or somehow remember who I am since I log in on the same computer each time.

I will definitely use them again for my fiction books, but I'm debating on my non-fiction works because they don't include any pictures for FreeTango, which means I have to buy their lowest package at $50.00. I know that's not much for some authors but for me, I'm a stay-at-home mom, so I can't justify the expense. I'd rather shop around and see if I can find someplace that will allow me to submit my own pictures for free, especially since I have less than 10.

~ Crystal Lee @CLeeAuthor

My point here is, choose wisely and follow the experience of others when you make a choice. Read a lot of reviews.

Places to Sell and Market Your Book

Sell:

http://www.smashwords.com/
https://kdp.amazon.com/self-publishing/signin
http://pubit.barnesandnoble.com/pubit_app/bn?t=pi_reg_home
https://www.createspace.com/
http://www.lulu.com
http://www.bookbaby.com/
http://www.apple.com/ibooks-author/
http://www.scribd.com/
http://www.booktango.com/

Market:

http://www.facebook.com
http://www.twitter.com
http://www.linkedin.com
http://www.wordpress.com
http://www.blogger.com

Section Six –
If Your Book is a Print Version

This is going to be the longest section of this book. If you give a crap what your book looks like in print, keep reading. If you want to look like a professional, keep reading. If you could care less, read none of this and struggle through on your own. If I were you, I'd read this and commit it to memory.

Before you start this section, go to http://www.createspace.com or your choice of print publisher and sign up for an account, click start a new project on your member dashboard, then let's get going. You need that reference open as we go through these steps. There are handy-dandy links you'll need to follow.

Remember, if you've followed the sections before this one, you'll already have most of this done. Some companies require pages in a different order! This is for CreateSpace versions only.

Your Book's Guts

Order of Pages

- Title page
- Copyright page
- Dedication page and/or author's note (if you have one)
- Table of Contents page

Ready to Retrieve the Formatted Word Document

Once you begin your new project, CreateSpace gives you all the tools you need to ensure your book rolls off their presses looking like a million bucks. Let's get started!

1. Open your book in Microsoft Word.
2. Go to CreateSpace and click on Add New Title. Fill in the name of the project and select paperback. Then choose a Guided setup process. You may be able to choose Streamlined *after* you read this book, but for now just choose Guided.
3. Now, fill in the next form completely and click Save and Continue.
4. ISBN choices! If you have an ISBN (you can't use one from a digital version and you can't use a free one from another website – like Smashwords), enter it here. Otherwise, click free CreateSpace assigned ISBN and let's move forward.
5. Copy your ISBN 10 and ISBN 13, paste it into a Notepad or separate Word document, and save it in your book's folder. Go paste it onto the bottom of your copyright page as well.

When you've completed these steps, CreateSpace will want to know what size you want your book printed at. Now, here's something you need to think about very carefully. A standard paperback is 5.5" x 8.5" but if your manuscript is bordering on 130K+ words, you might want to go up a size to 6" x 9" just to accommodate the gutter (part of the page inside the bound spine) and keep your book under 800 pages.

There's a little section under where you select the size of your book that has a Word document icon and two little blue links you're going to need. One is blank template and the other is formatted template. I want you to click the blank template link and tell the window that pops up to open it in MS Word.

1. Copy/Paste your book into the document.
2. Save it in your folder labeled CreateSpace in the sub-folder labeled with your book's title.
3. Press Ctrl+A to select all the text, go up top in MS Word where there are two As with the words Change Styles and click the drop-down arrow. Go to Style Sets and change the style to manuscript.
4. Do NOT deselect the text! If you did, hit Ctrl+A once again.
5. Click the font color button and select black.
6. Click the font choice and select your chosen font. *Leave the size button alone, please.*
7. Again, do NOT deselect the text, please!

8. Click the arrow on the bottom right corner of the section labeled **Paragraph** and look at the window that pops up. This is your paragraph panel. I will only say this once.
9. Under General: **Alignment** should be left and **Outline Level** should be body text.
10. Under Indentation: **Left** should be 0" **Right** should be 0" **Special** should be First Line **at** 0.3"
11. Under Spacing: **Before** should be 0pt **After** should be either 3pt or 6pt **Line Spacing** should be set to 1.5 lines and the **at** box should be blank.
12. Deselect your text.

CreateSpace is trying to help you look more professional with their template, but it will cause *you* more problems than you need while trying to format the book the way we want it. Because you were smart enough to buy this book, you know what you're doing. What you just downloaded was a sized document you can tweak to suit your purposes. How nice of them. Remember to tell them thank you for providing you with the basics (margins intact!).

Go reformat your title, copyright, dedication, and table of contents pages, and remove hyperlinks created for your digital version, we need all the text to print in black, please. Select each chapter heading and open your paragraph panel. Set the number under **Special** (where it says **First Line**) to none if your chapter headings are centered. If they are aligned left, leave them alone if you choose. This is a visual preference. See which one you like and go with it.

Orphans and Widows

Orphans and widows are those little bits of paragraphs or single words that are left on a page before or after a break. For clarification, here's an example:

At the bottom of a page:
When she walked through the room, she felt the carpet under

On the next page at the top:
her feet.
After she picked up the remote control and changed the channel, she allowed herself to fall back into the comfy confines of her oversized couch.

Now, I'm sure you can see the problems there. We need to get the words: her feet. on the preceding page with their counterparts: When she walked through the room, she felt the carpet under. We also need to get the word: couch. into the preceding paragraph.

We will start by picking up the word: couch.

1. Look at the **Font** section at the top of Word and click the little arrow to open the Font panel.
2. Click on the second tab labeled **Character Spacing**.
3. *Don't change anything except the following:*
4. Set **Spacing** to Condensed.
5. Click the up arrow next to 1.0pt until it reads 0.1pt.
6. Click OK.
7. If the word didn't jump up, repeat the above, changing the setting to 0.2pt.
8. Keep repeating those steps until the word couch jumps up. Don't go higher than 0.4pt.
9. If you've gone to 0.4pt and it still hasn't moved, change Spacing to Expanded and click the down arrow to bring it to 0.1pt.
10. Repeat until another word flows down and joins the word: couch.

Now, let's pick up the other pesky problem of the words: her feet.

1. Select all the text on the preceding page and open your paragraph panel again.
2. Change **After** to one number less than it is currently. If it's at 6, change it to 5, etc…
3. Click OK.
4. If the words didn't jump back a page, repeat and go down two numbers, then three, etc… until they do.

After you repair the issues, your text will flow like this:

At the bottom of a page:

When she walked through the room, she felt the carpet under her feet.

On the next page at the top:

After she picked up the remote control and changed the channel, she allowed herself to fall back into the comfy confines of her oversized couch.

Repeat the process for every lone word or lone partial paragraph you find. If your paragraph breaks and two sentences are on the next page, leave them alone, please.

Sometimes, the first sentence is on the preceding page. Just go add a page break and jump it to the next page. You can add manual page breaks in MS Word by clicking Ctrl+Enter.

Remember that text wrapped around photos looks great *if* it all lines up. Make sure it lines up!

When you're done working your text to make it very professional looking with the steps above, move on to the next section.

Pesky Page Numbers

Page numbers are a little tricky to get right in Word. I'll walk you through and hope you come out unscathed on the other side. No guarantees.

1. Place your cursor on the bottom of the page *before* the page where you want your numbers to begin.
2. Click the **Page Layout** tab and see the panel for **Page Setup**.
3. On the right-hand side, there's a little icon with the word **Breaks** next to it. Click the arrow and select **Next** (first option in the lower section).
4. Hit the Delete key 1x to get your page to jump back to your cursor.
5. Click the **Insert** tab.
6. Click **Footer**.
7. Choose **Blank**.
8. You'll now be in the **Design** tab.
9. In the **Navigation panel** click **link to previous**.
10. In the **Options panel**, make sure only **Show Document Text** has a check mark in the box.
11. Click **Page Number** and go down to **Current Position**.
12. Choose where and how you want your number to appear.
13. Click **Page Number** again and go to **Format Page Numbers**.
14. Select the radio button next to **Start on Page** and type a 1 in the box.

If you have an about the author page (if you don't, you really should) you need to repeat the page break process above through step 9. That will remove the page number.

If you realize how this process works and use it to maximum benefit, you'll be adding page numbers that flow beautifully to all sorts of things before long.

Things to remember:

- ✓ Page 1 is *always* on the right hand side (use manual page breaks to get it there).
- ✓ A running header (next topic) does not appear *any* page before 2.
- ✓ Running headers do not appear on chapter pages.

Running Headers

A running header is the text that appears at the top of a page that gives the author and title information. Generally, the author's name is on the even pages, and the title of the work is on the odd pages.

They never *ever* appear on the Chapter pages or *any* page before 2. I know I've said that already, but you need to hear it again and again. *You break the headers the same way you did the pages for the page numbers.* This may require some tweaking of the page numbers like going back to the format page numbers panel and clicking on continue from previous.

Be sure you have the box checked next to **different odd and even pages** under the **options** panel when adding your header. Make *sure* that you break the book where you need to (before and after every chapter page) so the header doesn't appear where it shouldn't.

I know it takes time. I know it's a PITA. Trust me, it's worth it.

Now that you've done all of the above, it's time to ***upload to CreateSpace*** and use their digital proofer to make sure everything appears just the way you wanted it to. If it doesn't, go back and start again from the first step. Please go page-by-page and look at each one.

Write down how many pages Word says you have from title page to your About the Author page. Do NOT go by page numbers you inserted for a page count. You'll be off.

Be amazed at what you just did!

Cover Considerations

Time for some good news! You already built your cover to fit the front of your book! Yay! Now it's as easy as grabbing the pre-made file from CreateSpace, opening it in your chosen image editor, and placing your cover file. Let's go get that file!

After you approve the digital proof of your book's guts:

1. Click **save and continue**.
2. Click **upload a print-ready PDF cover**.
3. Click the link in the sentence that is blue and says **submission requirements**.
4. Scroll about halfway down the page to the link right above the number three bullet that says **Download Cover Templates**.
5. Fill in the appropriate boxes with the information I had you gather earlier. Ah HA!
6. Save the zip file to your CreateSpace folder in the sub folder with your book title.
7. Unzip it.
8. Open Adobe Photoshop.

You may thank me now. You're welcome.

Follow these steps to complete your cover design with the provided template:

1. Click on **Open**.
2. Find the PDF you just downloaded from CreateSpace in your folder for your book.
3. Click on **New Layer**.
4. Click on the layer with your PDF guide on it and drag it above the new layer.

5. Click on **opacity** and drag the slider to 50%.
6. Click the **lock icon** on the top of the layers panel to prevent unwanted changes for the PDF layer.
7. Click on your new layer (the empty one).
8. Click on **Open**.
9. Open your cover file.
10. Make sure your layers are flattened then grab the **move tool** and drag your cover to the PDF guide document.
11. Close your cover file. Do NOT save changes.
12. If your cover file is already in CMYK, no need to change it. But if not, go to the section titled conversion to CMYK for further instructions.
13. Click NO when it asks if you want to flatten the layers.
14. Proceed to design your cover in the way you see fit. Follow the next heading (**Explaining Bleed and Safety**) to avoid creation errors that will cut off your artwork or lettering when your project is printed.
15. **Save** the file as a .psd in your CreateSpace folder for the book.
16. Turn off the visibility for the guide layer (click **the eye** that is in the side margin next to the layer).
17. Flatten your image. Say **yes** to discarding hidden layers.
18. **Save as** a .pdf with the following selections:
    ➢ Click OK when you get the box letting you know your settings can override current settings.
    ➢ Under **Adobe PDF Preset** click the drop down and choose [**PDF/X-1a:2001**].
    ➢ Under General, leave it alone.

> ➢ Under Compression choose Bicubic Downsampling to and set the numbers at 300 pixels/inch in the top box and 450 pixels/inch in the bottom. Compression should be set to JPEG and quality should be set to maximum.
> ➢ Under **Output>Color** set color output to **convert to destination**. **Destination** should be set to **U.S. Web Coated (SWOP) v2**.
> ➢ Under **PDF/X>Output Intent Profile Name** select **U.S. Web Coated (SWOP) v2**.
> ➢ Leave the rest alone.
> ➢ Check your summary and click **SAVE PDF**. Of course, in the CreateSpace folder.

Go upload that bad boy!

Explaining Bleed and Safety

You need images for me to explain what bleed and safety are. Again, images and e-books are not kind bedfellows. Go grab a look at this page:

http://jomichaels.blogspot.com/2012/05/design-lesson-number-2-printing.html

If you have a book that has spine area available, design inside the WHITE space, just like I showed you on that page.

I will now give you design definitions…

Bleed: The area that goes outside the printable area (it will be cut off)

Safety: The area in which you may put elements (white, usually) that will never be cut off.

Why the need for these? For a bleed, if you have a picture or snazzy background it needs to not have white space between it and the edge of the book. For a safety, printing presses are sometimes off by as much as 1/8" so there's no guarantee that your book cover will print exactly on the lines. You need a 1/8" bleed all the way around and a 1/8" safety inside the cut area. Just follow the guides and you'll be okay.

Uh oh… the dreaded *Things to Avoid*:

No borders around the edges of your book. If you have wide bands of color that cross over, make sure they bleed off the edges and are well inside your safety. Your borders will NOT be even. If you want flourishes, put them well inside your safety. Don't break that pink edge unless you don't care if you lose it and it doesn't have to be a consistent size.

Again, DON'T BREAK THAT PINK EDGE UNLESS YOU DON'T CARE IF YOU LOSE AND IT DOESN'T HAVE TO BE A CONSISTENT SIZE!

Anything that breaks the pink, needs to go all the way to the edge. It *will* be cut! Got it?

Conversion to CMYK for print

RULE #1: DO NOT USE PMS COLORS. If you don't know what I mean, GOOD. Moving on…

If you designed your book cover for the web or an e-reader, you'll have designed in RGB color space. RGB doesn't print. Printers use CMYK.

RGB: Red, Green, and Blue. Uses light to create color. Blend all three and you get white.

CMYK: Cyan, Magenta, Yellow, and Black. Uses ink to create color. Blend all four and you get a damned mess.

Your beautiful RGB colors won't look so hot in CMYK. They'll look gorgeous on a reading device, but when you print them, they look dull and/or muddy. Why did we convert before we saved the PDF? So you could see where your colors might need to be tweaked a bit for printing. Showing something with light is very different than showing something with ink. Look here for an example:

http://jomichaels.blogspot.com/2012/05/design-lesson-number-3-color-spaces.html

Layers (remember those pesky things?) were so you could go and tweak the individual elements or images without messing up all the others in the process.

You may thank me now.

LAB color: don't use it. Ever. You're designing a book cover.

HEXDEC: this color system is used on the web. It's the series of letters (A-F) and numbers (0-6) that are used to display a color on the WEB. Here's an interesting link:

http://www.december.com/html/spec/colorsafecodes.html

And now you have an idea of what colors are interchangeable.

PMS: spot colors. These are expensive because they do not use the four-color process of CMYK. Each color must be loaded individually and the paper run through the press again. You get charged for each run. Yikes! Just don't do it.

Math Involved

Just in case you need a bigger headache, you can mathematically figure out how to set up your own project without using the template so generously provided by CreateSpace. If you're that brave, go for it. I prefer ease and speed. But if you must know how to figure it yourself, read on:

If you have a book with a Black and White interior and white paper, calculate the spine width by multiplying your page count by 0.002252 and get your answer. So, if your book is 459 pages long, is B&W on white paper, your spine width will be 1.034"

Your document's width should be set up by adding together the following:

- ✓ Back Cover Trim Size
- ✓ Spine Width
- ✓ Front Cover Trim Size
- ✓ Bleed (.25" or .125" all the way around the outside])

So, for a 5.5" x 8.5" book with a spine width of 1.034", your math should look like this:

5.5 + 5.5 + 1.034 + .25 = 12.28" for the WIDTH of your document.

For the height, we know it's 8.5" plus bleed. So:

8.5 + .25 = 8.75" for the HEIGHT of your document.

For a color interior book, use 0.002347 for the multiplication of the spine width. If you're using cream paper, yet another number at 0.0025.

Setting up a Document from Scratch

Yes, you've goaded me into it. I'll tell you, but you aren't going to like it.

Here's how to not screw up when setting up your document in Adobe Photoshop:

1. Choose **New**.
2. Make sure you're set to **inches** and *not* **pixels**.
3. Type your previously figured out measurements into the proper boxes.
4. Make sure you're set to **330 pixels/inch** at a *minimum*.
5. Make sure your background is set to *transparent*.
6. Click **OK**.
7. Click **Ctrl+R** to show guides/rulers.
8. Grab your move tool and click inside the ruler on the left. Drag a guide (blue line) to .125" on the left side and repeat to drag another to 12.155" on the right side. That's your BLEED line (what will be cut off no matter what). **Math:** *12.28" - .125" = 12.155"*
9. Click inside the ruler on the top. Drag a guide to .125" on the top and another to 8.625" on the bottom. That's your BLEED line again (what will be cut off no matter what). **Math:** *8.75" - .125" = 8.625"*
10. Drag another guide to .25" on the left and to 12.03" on the right. Inside that is your SAFETY (what is safe from the cutting machine).
11. Drag yet another guide to .25" on the top and one to 8.5" on the bottom. Inside that is your SAFETY (what is safe from the cutting machine).
12. Drag yet another guide to 5.625" and another to 6.659". Those are your FOLDS for the spine. **Math:** *5.5" + .125" = 5.625"* That's your trim size and bleed on the back cover. **Math:** *5.5" +.125" + 1.034" = 6.659"* That's your trim size, bleed, and spine width.

13. Drag four more guides to **5.5"**, **5.75"**, **6.534"**, and **6.784"**. Inside those are your SAFETY area (what is safe from being mangled by the fold). **Math:** *5.625"-.125" = 5.5"* is your trim size and a 1/4" off your fold. **Math:** *5.5" + .125" = 5.75"* that's your fold location plus 1/8". **Math:** *6.659" - .125" = 6.534"* is your trim size, bleed, and spine size minus 1/8". **Math:** *6.659" + .125" = 6.784"* is your trim size, bleed, and spine width plus 1/8". In other words, any trim or fold needs at least a 1/8" safety (1/8" or .125").

14. You may remove the guides at **5.625"** and **6.659"** at this time. I do that because I'm not concerned where it folds after I know in what area I can add design elements.

15. Go to **Menu>View>Lock Guides**.

16. Remember the rules in the earlier section of this book and design away.

I hope you got all that. As I said, I prefer someone else to do it for me. Not because I can't do it, but because it's just easier. Now you know how to do it. Aren't you feeling super smart?

Afterword

I hope you have enjoyed your journey with me through design land. If you don't feel like doing any of this, you can contact me and I will happily do it for you – for a fee, of course. I also design logos, identity packages, and other such things. All of my photography is my own, of course, and you get no hidden charges.

You may find me on Twitter @WriteJoMichaels and I'll answer your questions as best as I can in 160 characters or less. *Joking...* Find me on Twitter and I'll send you my contact information and a rate card for my design services. I need to be sure you're a human and I loathe spam.

Feel free to connect with me on my blog! Follow me for future great tips about design stuff or writing stuff or a lot of stuff in general. I also write great stories and you can find a list of my books here:

http://jomichaels.blogspot.com/p/links-to-books.html

I hope I saved your hair and your forehead a lot of abuse with *The Indie Author's Guide to Building a Great Book*!

Well, that's it for this book, folks. Until next time, WRITE ON!

Jo

www.ingramcontent.com/pod-product-compliance
Lightning Source LLC
Chambersburg PA
CBHW060006300526
45794CB00003B/1112